BENJAMIN FRANKLIN'S
BOOK
OF
VIRTUES

PETER PAUPER PRESS, INC.
RYE BROOK, NEW YORK

PETER PAUPER PRESS
Fine Books and Gifts Since 1928

Our Company

In 1928, at the age of twenty-two, Peter Beilenson began printing books on a small press in the basement of his parents' home in Larchmont, New York. Peter—and later, his wife, Edna—sought to create fine books that sold at "prices even a pauper could afford."

Today, still family owned and operated, Peter Pauper Press continues to honor our founders' legacy—and our customers' expectations—of beauty, quality, and value.

One of America's most illustrious Founding Fathers, Benjamin Franklin (1706–1790) was also a printer, publisher, writer, postmaster, scientist, inventor, and diplomat.

Benjamin Franklin devised his personal "Plan for Attaining Moral Perfection" with his essential 13 virtues, and incorporated it into his memoirs, first published in 1791. The text for this *Book of Virtues* was excerpted from the 1916 Henry Holt and Company edition of *The Autobiography of Benjamin Franklin*, edited by Frank Woodworth Pine.

Cover image adapted from a binding by Alice Cordelia Morse
for *Tales of Two Countries*. The Metropolitan Museum of Art, New York,
Gift of Alice C. Morse, 1923, transferred from the Library

Designed by Margaret Rubiano

This edition copyright © 2025
Peter Pauper Press, Inc.
3 International Drive
Rye Brook, NY 10573

Published in the UK and Europe by Peter Pauper Press, Inc.
c/o White Pebble International
Units 2-3, Spring Business Park
Stanbridge Road
Havant, Hampshire PO9 2GJ, UK

Visit us at www.peterpauper.com

BENJAMIN FRANKLIN'S
BOOK
OF
VIRTUES

PLAN FOR ATTAINING MORAL PERFECTION

T WAS ABOUT this time I conceived the bold and arduous project of arriving at moral perfection. I wish'd to live without committing any fault at any time; I would conquer all that either natural inclination, custom, or company might lead me into. As I knew, or thought I knew, what was right and wrong, I did not see why I might not *always* do the one and avoid the other. But I soon found I had undertaken a task of more difficulty than I had imagined. While my care was employ'd in guarding against one fault, I was often surpris'd by another; habit took the advantage of inattention; inclination was sometimes too strong for reason. I concluded, at length, that the mere speculative conviction that it was our interest to be completely virtuous, was not sufficient to prevent our slipping; and that the contrary habits must be broken, and good ones acquir'd and establish'd, before we can have any dependence on a steady, uniform rectitude of conduct. For this purpose I therefore contrived the following method.

IN THE VARIOUS ENUMERATIONS OF THE MORAL VIRTUES I had met with in my reading, I found the catalogue more or less numerous, as different writers included more or fewer ideas under the same name. Temperance, for example, was by some confined to eating and drinking, while by others it was extended to mean the moderating every other pleasure, appetite, inclination, or passion, bodily or mental, even to our avarice and ambition. I propos'd to myself, for the sake of clearness, to use rather more names, with fewer ideas annex'd to each, than a few names with more ideas; and I included under thirteen names of virtues all that at that time occurr'd to me as necessary or desirable, and annex'd to each a short precept, which fully express'd the extent I gave to its meaning.

These names of virtues, with their precepts, were:

1.
TEMPERANCE

Eat not to dullness.
Drink not to elevation.

2.
SILENCE

Speak not but what may benefit others or yourself.
Avoid trifling conversation.

3.
ORDER

Let all your things have their places.
Let each part of your business have its time.

4.
RESOLUTION

Resolve to perform what you ought.
Perform without fail what you resolve.

5.
FRUGALITY

Make no expense but to do good to others
or yourself; *i.e.,* waste nothing.

6.
INDUSTRY

Lose no time.
Be always employ'd in something useful.
Cut off all unnecessary actions.

7.
SINCERITY

Use no hurtful deceit.
Think innocently and justly; and, if you speak,
speak accordingly.

8.
JUSTICE

Wrong none by doing injuries, or omitting the
benefits that are your duty.

9.
MODERATION

Avoid extremes.
Forbear resenting injuries so much as you think
they deserve.

10.
CLEANLINESS

Tolerate no uncleanliness in body, clothes,
or habitation.

11.
TRANQUILITY

Be not disturbed at trifles, or at accidents
common or unavoidable.

12.
CHASTITY

Rarely use venery but for health or offspring;
never to dullness, weakness, or the injury of your own
or another's peace or reputation.

13.

HUMILITY

Imitate Jesus and Socrates.

While my care was employ'd in guarding against one fault, I was often surpris'd by another; habit took the advantage of inattention; inclination was sometimes too strong for reason. I concluded, at length, that the mere speculative conviction that it was our interest to be completely virtuous, was not sufficient to prevent our slipping; and that the contrary habits must be broken, and good ones acquir'd and establish'd, before we can have any dependence on a steady, uniform rectitude of conduct.

Y INTENTION BEING TO ACQUIRE THE *HABITUDE* OF ALL THESE VIRTUES, I judg'd it would be well not to distract my attention by attempting the whole at once, but to fix it on one of them at a time; and, when I should be master of that, then to proceed to another, and so on, till I should have gone thro' the thirteen; and, as the previous acquisition of some might facilitate the acquisition of certain others, I arrang'd them with that view, as they stand above. *Temperance* first, as it tends to procure that coolness and clearness of head, which is so necessary where constant vigilance was to be kept up, and guard maintained against the un-remitting attraction of ancient habits, and the force of perpetual temptations. This being acquir'd and estab-lish'd, *Silence* would be more easy; and my desire being to gain knowledge at the same time that I improv'd in virtue, and considering that in conversation it was obtain'd rather by the use of the ears than of the tongue, and therefore wishing to break a habit I was getting into of prattling, punning, and joking, which only made me acceptable to trifling company, I gave *Silence* the second place. This and the next, *Order*, I expected would allow me more time for attending to my project and my studies. *Resolution*, once become habitual, would keep

me firm in my endeavors to obtain all the subsequent virtues; *Frugality* and *Industry* freeing me from my remaining debt, and producing affluence and independence, would make more easy the practice of *Sincerity* and *Justice*, etc., etc. Conceiving then, that, agreeably to the advice of Pythagoras in his *Golden Verses*[1], daily examination would be necessary, I contrived the following method for conducting that examination.

I MADE A LITTLE BOOK, in which I allotted a page for each of the virtues. I rul'd each page with red ink, so as

to have seven columns, one for each day of the week, marking each column with a letter for the day. I cross'd these columns with thirteen red lines, marking the beginning of each line with the first letter of one of the virtues, on which line, and in its proper column, I might mark, by a little black spot, every fault I found upon examination to have been committed respecting that virtue upon that day.

FORM OF THE PAGES

TEMPERANCE
Eat not to dullness.
Drink not to elevation.

	Sun	M	T	W	Th	F	S
TEMPERANCE							
SILENCE							
ORDER							
RESOLUTION							
FRUGALITY							
INDUSTRY							
SINCERITY							
JUSTICE							
MODERATION							
CLEANLINESS							
TRANQUILITY							
CHASTITY							
HUMILITY							

 DETERMINED to give a week's strict attention to each of the virtues successively. Thus, in the first week, my great guard was to avoid every the least offense against *Temperance*, leaving the other virtues to their ordinary chance, only marking every evening the faults of the day. Thus, if in the first week I could keep my first line, marked T, clear of spots, I suppos'd the habit of that virtue so much strengthen'd, and its opposite weaken'd, that I might venture extending my attention to include the next, and for the following week keep both lines clear of spots. Proceeding thus to the last, I could go thro' a course complete in thirteen weeks, and four courses in a year. And like him who, having a garden to weed, does not attempt to eradicate all the bad herbs at once, which would exceed his reach and his strength, but works on one of the beds at a time, and, having accomplish'd the first, proceeds to a second, so I should have, I hoped, the encouraging pleasure of seeing on my pages the progress I made in virtue, by clearing successively my lines of their spots, till in the end, by a number of courses, I should be happy in viewing a clean book, after a thirteen weeks' daily examination.

This my little book had for its motto these lines from Addison's *Cato*:

*"Here will I hold. If there's a power above us
(And that there is, all nature cries aloud
Thro' all her works), He must delight in virtue;
And that which he delights in must be happy."*

Another from Cicero,

> *"O vitæ Philosophia dux! O virtutum indagatrix expultrixque vitiorum! Unus dies, bene et ex præceptis tuis actus, peccanti immortalitati est anteponendus."* [2]

Another from the Proverbs of Solomon, speaking of wisdom or virtue:

> *"Length of days is in her right hand, and in her left hand riches and honour. Her ways are ways of pleasantness, and all her paths are peace."* III. 16, 17.

And conceiving God to be the fountain of wisdom, I thought it right and necessary to solicit his assistance for obtaining it; to this end I formed the following little prayer, which was prefix'd to my tables of examination, for daily use.

> *"O powerful Goodness! bountiful Father! merciful Guide! Increase in me that wisdom which discovers my truest interest. Strengthen my resolutions to perform what that wisdom dictates. Accept my kind offices to thy other children as the only return in my power for thy continual favours to me."*

I used also sometimes a little prayer which I took from Thomson's Poems, viz.:

> "Father of light and life, thou Good Supreme!
> O teach me what is good; teach me Thyself!
> Save me from folly, vanity, and vice,
> From every low pursuit; and fill my soul
> With knowledge, conscious peace, and virtue pure;
> Sacred, substantial, never-fading bliss!"

I ENTER'D UPON THE EXECUTION OF THIS PLAN FOR SELF-EXAMINATION, and continu'd it with occasional intermissions for some time. I was surpris'd to find myself so much fuller of faults than I had imagined; but I had the satisfaction of seeing them diminish. To avoid the trouble of renewing now and then my little book, which, by scraping out the marks on the paper of old faults to make room for new ones in a new course, became full of holes, I transferr'd my tables and precepts to the ivory leaves of a memorandum book, on which the lines were drawn with red ink, that made a durable stain, and on those lines I mark'd my faults with a black-lead pencil, which marks I could easily wipe out with a wet sponge. After a while I went thro' one course only in a year, and afterward only one in several years, till at length I omitted them entirely, being employ'd in voyages and business abroad, with a multiplicity of affairs that interfered; but I always carried my little book with me.

MY SCHEME OF *ORDER* gave me the most trouble; and I found that, tho' it might be practicable where a man's business was such as to leave him the disposition of his time, that of a journeyman printer, for instance, it was not possible to be exactly observed by a master, who must mix with the world, and often receive people of

business at their own hours. *Order*, too, with regard to places for things, papers, etc., I found extremely difficult to acquire. I had not been early accustomed to it, and, having an exceeding good memory, I was not so sensible of the inconvenience attending want of method. This article, therefore, cost me so much painful attention, and my faults in it vexed me so much, and I made so little progress in amendment, and had such frequent relapses, that I was almost ready to give up the attempt, and content myself with a faulty character in that respect, like the man who, in buying an ax of

may attend the remainder is in the hand of Providence; but, if they arrive, the reflection on past happiness enjoy'd ought to help his bearing them with more resignation. To *Temperance* he ascribes his long-continu'd health, and what is still left to him of a good constitution; to *Industry* and *Frugality*, the early easiness of his circumstances and acquisition of his fortune, with all that knowledge that enabled him to be a useful citizen, and obtain'd for him some degree of reputation among the learned; to *Sincerity* and *Justice*, the confidence of his country, and the honorable employs it conferred upon him; and to the joint influence of the whole mass of the virtues, even in the imperfect state he was able to acquire them, all that evenness of temper, and that cheerfulness in conversation, which makes his company still sought for, and agreeable even to his younger acquaintance. I hope, therefore, that some of my descendants may follow the example and reap the benefit.

It will be remark'd that, tho' my scheme was not wholly without religion, there was in it no mark of any of the distinguishing tenets of any particular sect. I had purposely avoided them; for, being fully persuaded of the utility and excellency of my method, and that it might be serviceable to people in all religions, and intending some time or other to publish it, I would not

have anything in it that should prejudice anyone, of any sect, against it. I purposed writing a little comment on each virtue, in which I would have shown the advantages of possessing it, and the mischiefs attending its opposite vice; and I should have called my book *The Art of Virtue*, because it would have shown the means and manner of obtaining virtue, which would have distinguished it from the mere exhortation to be good, that does not instruct and indicate the means, but is like the apostle's man of verbal charity, who only without showing to the naked and hungry how or where they might get clothes or victuals, exhorted them to be fed and clothed. —*James* II. 15, 16.

But it so happened that my intention of writing and publishing this comment was never fulfilled. I did, indeed, from time to time, put down short hints of the sentiments, reasonings, etc., to be made use of in it, some of which I have still by me; but the necessary close attention to private business in the earlier part of my life, and public business since, have occasioned my postponing it; for, it being connected in my mind with *a great and extensive project*, that required the whole man to execute, and which an unforeseen succession of employs prevented my attending to, it has hitherto remain'd unfinish'd.

IN THIS PIECE IT WAS MY DESIGN to explain and enforce this doctrine, that vicious actions are not hurtful because they are forbidden, but forbidden because they are hurtful, the nature of man alone considered; that it was, therefore, everyone's interest to be virtuous who wish'd to be happy even in this world; and I should, from this circumstance (there being always in the world a number of rich merchants, nobility, states, and princes, who have need of honest instruments for the

management of their affairs, and such being so rare), have endeavoured to convince young persons that no qualities were so likely to make a poor man's fortune as those of probity and integrity.

My list of virtues contain'd at first but twelve; but a Quaker friend having kindly informed me that I was generally thought proud; that my pride show'd itself frequently in conversation; that I was not content with being in the right when discussing any point, but was overbearing, and rather insolent, of which he convinc'd me by mentioning several instances; I determined endeavouring to cure myself, if I could, of this vice or folly among the rest, and I added *Humility* to my list, giving an extensive meaning to the word.

I cannot boast of much success in acquiring the *reality* of this virtue, but I had a good deal with regard to the *appearance* of it. I made it a rule to forbear all direct contradiction to the sentiments of others, and all positive assertion of my own. I even forbid myself, agreeably to the old laws of our Junto, the use of every word or expression in the language that imported a fix'd opinion, such as *certainly, undoubtedly*, etc., and I adopted, instead of them, *I conceive, I apprehend*, or *I imagine* a thing to be so or so; or it *so appears to me*

at present. When another asserted something that I
thought an error, I deny'd myself the pleasure of con-
tradicting him abruptly, and of showing immediately
some absurdity in his proposition; and in answering
I began by observing that in certain cases or circumstances his opinion would be right, but in the present
case there *appear'd* or *seem'd* to me some difference,
etc. I soon found the advantage of this change in my
manner; the conversations I engag'd in went on more
pleasantly. The modest way in which I propos'd my
opinions procur'd them a readier reception and less
contradiction; I had less mortification when I was
found to be in the wrong, and I more easily prevail'd
with others to give up their mistakes and join with me
when I happened to be in the right.

And this mode, which I at first put on with some
violence to natural inclination, became at length so
easy, and so habitual to me, that perhaps for these
fifty years past no one has ever heard a dogmatical
expression escape me. And to this habit (after my
character of integrity) I think it principally owing that
I had early so much weight with my fellow-citizens
when I propos'd new institutions, or alterations in the
old, and so much influence in public councils when I
became a member; for I was but a bad speaker, never

eloquent, subject to much hesitation in my choice of words, hardly correct in language, and yet I generally carried my points.

IN REALITY, there is, perhaps, no one of our natural passions so hard to subdue as *pride*. Disguise it, struggle with it, beat it down, stifle it, mortify it as much as one pleases, it is still alive, and will every now and then peep out and show itself; you will see it, perhaps, often in this history; for, even if I could conceive that I had completely overcome it, I should probably be proud of my humility.

But, on the whole, tho' I never arrived at the perfection I had been so ambitious of obtaining, but fell far short of it, yet I was, by the endeavour, a better and a happier man than I otherwise should have been if I had not attempted it.

NOTES

1 *Let not the stealing God of Sleep surprise,*
  Nor creep in Slumbers on thy weary Eyes,
  Ere ev'ry Action of the former Day,
  Strictly thou dost and righteously survey.
  With Rev'rence at thy own Tribunal stand,
  And answer justly to thy own Demand.
  Where have I been? In what have I transgress'd?
  What Good or Ill has this Day's Life express'd?
  Where have I fail'd in what I ought to do?
  In what to God, to Man, or to myself I owe?
  Inquire severe what-e'er from first to last,
  From Morning's Dawn 'till Ev'ning's Gloom, has past.
  If Evil were thy Deeds, repenting mourn,
  And let thy Soul with strong Remorse be torn.
  If Good, the Good with Peace of Mind repay,
  And to thy secret Self with Pleasure say,
  Rejoice, my Heart, for all went well today.

  —from the *Golden Verses,* traditionally attributed to
  the Pythagorean philosophers, translated by Nicholas
  Rowe

2 "O philosophy, guide of life! O searcher out of virtue
  and exterminator of vice! One day spent well and in
  accordance with thy precepts is worth an immortality
  of sin."
  —*Tusculan Inquiries*, Book V., translator unknown

ART CREDITS

Page 4 :
Engraving by Henry Bryan Hall (1868) from the
original painting by Joseph-Siffred Duplessis.
Courtesy of the United States Library of Congress

Page 6, Page 29 :
Quaint cuts by an unknown hand, from
Poor Richard's Almanack

Illustrations by E. Boyd Smith, from
The Autobiography of Benjamin Franklin:
Page 17: Early Friends in Philadelphia
Page 21: First Visit to London
Page 27: Plan for Attaining Moral Perfection
Page 32: Quarrels with the Proprietary Governors
Page 36: Franklin's Seal